St Ende

Prizi

CW01640650

Prizing the Passion

Four Lent Talks and Selected Poems

David Steven

~ F P ~
Firedint Publishing
Oxford

Copyright © David Steven 2024
Firedint Publishing Oxford
76 Kingston Road
Oxford OX2 6RJ
~ F P ~

David Steven asserts the moral right to be identified as the editor of this work in accordance with the Copyright, Designs and Patents Act 1988.
All rights reserved under International and Pan-American Copyright Conventions. No part of this publication may be reproduced, transmitted, downloaded or stored in a retrieval system by any means, electric, mechanical, photocopying or otherwise, without the express written permission of the publisher.

ISBN 978-1-9999407-6-8

August 2024

Contents

Four Lent Talks

Selected Poems

Acknowledgements

The four Lent talks were given at the Collegiate Church of St Endellion, North Cornwall, in 2011, and I warmly thank the clergy and church wardens for their invitation to me.

The poem 'Mount Grace Priory' was earlier printed in *Christians Aware*, Autumn 2022.

The poems 'The Mary Magdalene Frontal', 'In a Seaside Café at Gorran Haven', 'Child and Mother – Treliske Hospital', and 'Mrs Arnolfi Replies to her Husband' were earlier printed in *A Festivity of Love*, ed. Judith Pollinger and Paul S. Fiddes (Oxford: Firedint, 2018) and are reprinted by permission.

The poem by Charles Williams on page 38 is copyright ©Bruce Hunter and David Higham Associates in the USA, and is reproduced by kind permission.

The cover shows 'Christ Crowned with Thorns' by Hieronymus Bosch, 1479–1516, in the Collection of the National Gallery, London. The image is in the public domain in the UK and the USA and is reproduced from Wikimedia Commons.

Four Lent Talks

Introduction

'Tis death my soul to be indifferent;
Set forth thyself unto thy whole extent,
And all the glory of his Passion prize,
Who for thee lives, who for thee dies.
Thomas Traherne (1637–1674)[1]

Long have I known and loved these words: little have I lived them. From the moment of that discovery, early in my life, they have ebbed and flowed like the tide of the nearby sea, always there yet often neglected or forgotten. I do not have much verse known by heart, but these lines have been there for most of my adult life. As the most active part of life comes towards its end, the lines have taken on a persistence, almost a haunting quality, that can seem at times to question, if not my faith, then certainly to challenge my living-out of the same. Perhaps such lines are best seen as a marker at a junction of roads, to which I may return from time to time to take a new bearing, explore a new direction, follow a way that brings a new, even unwelcome, area of experience, or brings me up short before a barred gate that closes experience from me.

1

' 'Tis death, my soul, to be indifferent'

Traheme uses the word 'indifferent' in a very modern way. A more common seventeenth- century use of the word is found in the *Book of Common Prayer* in the 'Prayer for the Church' found in the Holy Communion Service. The congregation is asked to pray 'that the King's Council may truly and indifferently minister justice'. In the past I suppose many others substituted 'impartiality' for 'indifference', for that is what it means here, and in the most recent printing of the service this change is made. But Traherne uses 'indifference' in its modern sense, and challenges us to see it as the primary cause of the soul's death, in his time as in our own.

Much of the language of theology has become a foreign language to a huge swathe of Western society. It is not simply that long words like 'incarnation' and 'atonement' are not on the lips of the average and proverbial 'man on the street', nor are words such as 'grace' or 'faith'. Traherne, like other poets of his age, George Herbert, John Donne and others, can use a complex verbal construction that can seem a maze of words whose meaning must slowly be teased out by the reader. But here is no such complexity. No technical confusions, no involved imagery, nothing to shield us from the stark and frightening truth of his words. Nor can we draw comfort from the possibility that he means that indifference is simply or merely the cause of the death of the soul: that may indeed be a result of the indifference, but the death is the death of the whole person, and the soul is addressed as being that part of us that can grasp the enormity of our failure, and then find the strength to set out again on a path that takes us out of our indifference. The only way this is to be done is by our affirming, in life and in death, the glory of Christ's Passion.

Over the years I have found that the Old Testament has forced itself more and more upon me, phrases and themes coming out of great swathes of history, the countries of its origins filling pages of our newspapers and hours of radio and television. Egypt, Syria, Israel, Iraq (Mesopotamia, Syria and Babylon) and Iran. Above all, the Old Testament seems to me now a series of books that challenged the indifference of their own age, and too often, and too painfully, the indifference of our own. I should have known otherwise from the start. During the 1960s and 1970s about one tenth of England's Anglican clergy was trained at King's College, London, where their Old Testament lecturer was the imposing Dr Ulrich Simon, some of whose family had perished at Auschwitz. To this day I can remember laughing at the irrelevance of a book such as Leviticus, with all its rigmarole of what Jewish clergy were to wear and obscure observations about diet or building regulations. 'Cursed is he who removes his neighbour's landmark' seemed to sum up all that was pointless in the long Levitical legislative lists. We were not quite 'Swinging Sixties', staid young students maybe, but we were hearing Bishop John Robinson and reading his *Honest to God* on the tube.

How wrong could I be? Those were the years when the removal of a neighbour's landmark was common, a sign of the oppression of peoples and the removal of their rights to the land. The end of the Sixties saw me in South Africa, where the removal of peoples from their land and their homes was one of the results of Apartheid legislation, and I found myself ministering daily to people who had had their landmarks removed, their fields and farms given to others, their homes demolished and they and their families dumped on the arid wastelands of the Northern Cape. I dealt daily too with those who did the removing or who, at least, benefitted from it. The Old Testament came alive and its prophetic injunctions voiced the anger and frustration of the black and coloured people of the land. Some white South Africans were also angry. But Leviticus promises a curse, and South Africa's painful beauty is cursed with a high crime rate and an HIV/AIDS epidemic almost out of control, part of the fruit of a nation's indifference in the past and, as far as AIDS is concerned, the total indifference today of many African men towards women and girls: rape is common. Other landmarks in other places were removed: nations other than South Africa struggle with the bitter fruits of past policies. Canada and the USA in the treatment of (Native) Indians, New Zealand and the Maoris, Australia and its Aboriginal population. In the Holy Land, many Israelis are willing to risk the Levitical curse by removing the landmarks of the fields and homes, of the vineyards and the olive groves of their Palestinian neighbours.

The removal of landmarks showed indifference on a massive scale during the nineteenth and twentieth centuries. This century will have to repair the damage, which is not only what mainly 'white' people have done to mainly 'non-white', or colonial expansionists to indigenous peoples. The need to repair relationships, replace landmarks, make restitution, is a much wider need. The figures for deaths during Africa's civil wars are truly terrible, and the countries a litany of human shame. Most of them have been post-colonial wars: Angola, Congo, Sudan, Mozambique, Somalia, Zimbabwe. Corruption and bad governance could also lead us to despair of Africa ever 'coming right'. Millions have died in these civil wars, yet in some of the worst situations, the church , at best, 'the churches', have risen to desperate challenges and become an instrument of peace. This was notably so in Mozambique, and hopefully will continue to be so in Southern Sudan. The modern history of Africa raises one of the most difficult issues the Church faces, and the same is so for parts of South America, the Philippines, Burma, and in any country where serious forms of oppression are used by the State.

In his novel about Haiti, *The Comedians,* Graham Greene writes: 'The Church condemns violence, but it condemns indifference more harshly. Violence can be an expression of love, indifference never'.[2] This was exactly the issue that faced the church in South Africa during Apartheid. By 1970 almost all the legislation was in place: The Group Areas Act, The Job Reservation Act, The Immorality Act. When these combined, a man could lose his house, his job and his family at the stroke of an official's pen. Fifty leading South African Christian leaders wrote an open letter to the governing Nationalist Party accusing them of following the same policies as the National Socialist Party of Germany, the Nazis, in the 1930s. At the same time, the World Council of Churches started making grants to the African National Congress (ANC) in exile. These grants were for 'humanitarian purposes', but the average white South African was enraged. Those of us in the South African Council of Churches were accused of supporting violence, but at the same time the eighteen-year-old sons of my colleagues were conscripted into the South African Armed Forces, where, as one teenager put it to me, 'We are simply being trained to shoot Blacks'. The history of South Africa from 1947 to 1994 might well be written in terms of 'who was indifferent?' By their refusal to be indifferent to the plight of others, some paid with their lives. So it has always been. The Old Testament is full of cries for justice for the poor, the oppressed, for the widow and the orphans, and AIDS leaves South Africa with more than a million of these. Shakespeare's most famous speech touches on the inner conflict between indifference and action that may be violent:

> Whether 'tis nobler in the mind to suffer
> The slings and arrows of outrageous fortune,
> Or to take arms against a sea of troubles,
> And by opposing end them? (*Hamlet*, Act 3, Scene 1)

Almost all our hopes of the 'Arab Spring' are being drowned in a 'sea of troubles' of the most cruel and devastating kind.

We do not often see indifference, especially our own, as being on the same plane as violence, but others do. At the end of Part One of *Murder in the Cathedral,* T. S. Eliot has Thomas Becket, Archbishop of Canterbury, include 'indifference' among the evils of sacrilege, crime, oppression, exploitation and death at the blade of an axe. Becket warns those who hear him that for all these evils, *including indifference* 'You must all be punished'.[3] The Prayer Book is more gentle with us, but the impact is the same; 'We have left undone those things which we ought to have done, and we have done those things which we ought not to have done and there is no health in us.'

I referred earlier to many deaths from Africa's civil wars, and using Eliot's terms we can call them deaths at the axe's blade, but every year we 'allow' the death by indifference of tens of thousands of children, mostly under five, from malaria and from water-borne diseases. Having a good sewerage system—any sewerage system—should be high on every African Government's list of priorities, rather than guns, big cars and private jets. To what purpose is a land defended from external enemies if its own children die daily from dysentery? For many around the world a good well is wealth indeed. Indifference to these unnecessary deaths can be claimed against national leaders, but we have both some responsibility and some power as well. On an almost daily basis I get appeals and reminders from different charities on a vast range of vital projects, from tree planting to smoke-free ovens, from mine clearance to treating leprosy, against the use of torture or for adult literacy. How I am meant to prioritize these I have no idea. In Great Britain we have more than 10,000 charitable organizations, all wanting to challenge any indifference I may have left after all these mail shots. Perhaps the crisis in Haiti can point to some of the problems. Good governance, good administration, good organization in disaster response, these are the major players in the battle against indifference. And perhaps now is the time, when donations to many charities are going down, for more of them to be combined together, to limit administration costs and prevent what can too easily become a competitive market for 'doing good'. And we must be far more careful that the aid we contribute does not undermine or destroy local agriculture and markets, for that too is an act of indifference.

Indifference is complex. In Yorkshire, Nottinghamshire, South Wales one of the most distinct landmarks was the pit-head, the great wheel turning as men went into the depths of the earth on a dirty, dangerous and disease-ridden job, to mine the coal that fired the industrial revolution and economic prosperity. Whole communities were geared up to this way of life, and whole communities suffered when pits closed and little was there to take their place. A similar picture can be painted, and loss felt, in Yorkshire and Lancashire mill towns or Cornish fishing villages. We may feel that we have been indifferent to the pain of these communities, but we can too easily be indifferent to the people doing the mining and weaving now. In parts of South America children are mining coal: in parts of India children are weaving cloth. Indifference to their safety and their health would certainly place us alongside the rich man in the parable and the children with Lazarus at the gate.

When we look at the second line of Traherne's poem, 'set forth thyself unto thy whole extent', we shall see some of the remedies for any residual indifference, and in the glory of Christ's Passion we shall find our only healing; not ours alone, but of the world.

As we look out upon a world that often seems, as to Hamlet a 'sea of troubles', we are likely to feel overwhelmed by our inadequacy — 'but what can I do?' We can start by being encouraged by Shakespeare again, this time from *Julius Caesar* (Act IV, scene 3):

> There is a tide in the affairs of men,
> Which taken at the flood, leads on to fortune;
> Omitted, all the voyage of their life
> Is bound in shallows and in miseries.
> On such a full sea are we now afloat,
> And we must take the current when it serves,
> Or lose our ventures.

There is a haunting story of a man who missed his tide like this, who can remind us that indifference to ourselves and our potential can be as serious a fault as indifference to others. A great artist worked in Rome. He decided to set out on a huge painting of the Last Supper. He needed models for the thirteen men around the table. He found a fine looking man and arranged for him to be painted as Jesus. The work progressed slowly: he had to fulfil commissions in order to live, and only gradually did the other figures get painted. At last, years later he came to the final face—Judas Iscariot. He went out into the streets again and found a harsh, cruel, depraved face lurking in a doorway. Persuading him to come to the studio he began work. The man spoke: 'Don't you remember me?' 'I've never seen you before.' replied the artist indignantly. 'Oh yes you have. Years ago you painted me as the Christ, but you see, I've drifted.' Perhaps upon his own 'sea of troubles', unable to take any tide at its flood, life had led him not to fortune, but to the shallows and miseries of his present condition.

Not only do most of us know someone who has drifted in such a way, but we can probably see in our own lives, times or situations when we too were adrift, sometimes entirely at our own fault, at other times at the fault of other people. Perhaps most often, we see it as we struggle with illness and the failure of the health and wholeness we long for.

John Clare is one of our great poets, especially in his love for his

Northamptonshire countryside, but for a large part of his adult life, from 1837 until his death in 1864, he was confined to mental asylums. Few have captured self-despair and little hope or longing more succinctly or more movingly than Clare in his poem 'I am'. However, it also takes us into a different area: how we feel when others seem indifferent to us.

> I am—yet what I am none cares or knows;
> My friends forsake me like a memory lost:
> I am the self-consumer of my woes—
> They rise and vanish in oblivion's host.
> Like shadows in love frenzied stifled throes;
> And yet I am, and live—like vapours tost
> Into the nothingness of scorn and noise
> Into the living sea of waking dreams,
> Where there is neither sense of life nor joys,
> But the vast shipwreck of my life's esteems;
> Even the dearest that I loved the best
> Are strange—nay, rather stranger than the rest.
> I long for scenes where man hath never trod
> A place where woman never smiled or wept;
> There to abide with my creator, God,
> And sleep as I in childhood sweetly slept,
> Untroubling and untroubled where I lie
> The grass below, above the vaulted sky.[4]

Once again the sea is a central image, a sea of troubles, a tide of flood, of voyage and shipwreck. There is depressing illusion: Clare thought that not only was he all sorts of other people, but that no other person cared for who he really was. You do not have to be as sensitive as Clare to fear the indifference of others from time to time.

Traherne does not have an easy solution to worldly indifference, but he does point a way forward, a signpost to a way that might be for some, perhaps for many, a form of resolution: 'Set forth thyself unto thy whole extent'. We look at that phrase next, and in the meantime we should reflect upon the events of Christ's Passion that are so marked by indifference: the indifferent motives of the chief priests, the indifferent fickleness of the crowd, the indifference of Pilate as he washes his hands, the indifferent callousness of the soldiers as they carry out their duty. But we can do better; we can 'set forth ourselves unto our whole extent'. And we shall.

2

'Set forth thyself unto thy whole extent'

The history of the Christian church is filled with examples of people we admire because, in some small way, or else in some great course of action, they have indeed 'set forth themselves unto their whole extent'. We can look at the lives of early ascetics in the desert and soon realize that years in a cave is not for us. It is harder to see things closer to home, even in someone we know, to recognize that the difference between us and them is simply that they have 'set forth' more fully than we have. I remember Frank Smith, old and seriously crippled with arthritis, who struggled to the great parish church in the centre of town from his tiny house in a back street. I gave him a lift home once or twice, two up, two down, tiny rooms, one still lit by a gas mantle. From here he set 'set forth' each Sunday evening. Or a woman in a remote part of the Northern Cape in South Africa, who attended a Communion service I was taking in a house. I offered her a lift home, and noting the mileage, bumped along tracks and trails in the desert sands. The home from which she had 'set forth' on foot was ten miles away.

There can be no interpretation of the Christian faith and life that does not have sacrifice at its centre. All our 'setting forth' is rooted in the 'setting forth' of Jesus. 'He set his face towards Jerusalem' (Luke 9:53).

It is easy to get our 'setting forth' wrong, maybe by a vigorous Protestant work ethic that makes an endless and constant demand upon ourselves, until we are reduced to a constant striving that ends in breakdown. Or else by a rule and code of practice that is so strict that it cannot truly see the man lying beaten at the side of the road because a religious timetable is to be adhered to. Sometimes, of course, when we take on our Good Samaritan mantle, we can find ourselves reminded that there is more to be done. Soon after arriving in an African parish, a large and historic hotel was being sold up, and at the auction I not only furnished my home but bought a pile of blankets: the winter nights on the edge of the desert are bitterly cold. Giving a blanket to an African man some time later, he thanked me most warmly, adding that if I should ever have a spare bed to go with it, he would be most grateful. I had begun to 'set forth' but not gone very far!

There are some who are called to remarkable acts of sacrifice. Sometimes this occurs when well-trained people put their training into effect without pausing to count the cost. The firemen, ambulance crews and police who went into the Twin Towers in New York on 9/11/2001, whilst others streamed out, only to be killed themselves as the towers collapsed, are one such group along with the English security guard who remained to help those leaving, only to die himself. Amongst the head-breaking stories from the Queensland floods, is that of a boy of thirteen who insisted his younger brother be taken into the rescue boat first, only to be swept away himself a few moments later.

These are not necessarily religious people or religious acts, but they are people who—in a moment of extreme crisis—have made a costly judgement, and thus have 'set forth unto their whole extent', even of their lives. Ours is not an age where the word 'duty' is much used but 'setting forth ourselves' requires a concept of duty we must recover. If we are to challenge the indifference that can lead to death, faithfulness and duty are the bedrock of the challenge. It is sometimes easier to rise up with wings like eagles to meet a great challenge that comes to us, than it is to run and not be weary, to walk and not faint along the path of daily duty (Isaiah 40:31). I wonder more and more at the sort of love-in-duty that keeps a parent caring for a severely handicapped child, until the one is old and the other middle-aged, and I see it as the 'walk and not faint' that I could never achieve. Any government or local council that diminishes help for such people does not deserve to remain in power, and if it means some of us paying more tax as our duty so that such help can continue, then that is what should happen.

Recent examples of rising up like an eagle have been the Jubilee 2000 campaign, 'Make Poverty History', and the 'IF' programme to remove world hunger. But after the eagle bit comes the hard slog, the constant effort of nagging governments or pleading with congregations to keep up the momentum for years and years, for a world of fairer trade and unexploited lives. Jubilee 2000 stands as a powerful example to all who say either that the church should not get involved in this way, especially if it has anything to do with politics, or else that there is nothing we can usefully do. It should and there is!

The local congregation exists to be a centre of excellence against an often indifferent world. People should come through our church doors and find examples of good practice in the setting forth of ourselves 'unto our whole extent'. Too often the message we give is one of self-preservation rather than self-sacrifice. Too often we seem afraid of upsetting some local apple cart, when sadly few apples remain.

When I took on a large urban parish the church was almost immediately closed for major repairs: it was over a coal mine. I was very proud of what we eventually achieved, with our clean stone work, polished wood, re-ordered sanctuary, our re-hung bells, our choir and organ and our worship. But I felt prouder still when, some years later, I came into the church half-way through my sabbatical leave. The back pews were stuffed full of black bin bags which contained the clothes the parish had donated for Bosnian refugees, and the building was doing its share of the parish 'setting forth itself unto its whole extent'.

To this 'whole extent' we must turn, to what I would call a doctrine of Extension. It is the other side of the accepted doctrine of Intention. When a couple come to a church to get married, they marry each other; the priest, in taking the service, facilitates the process. This means that even if a bogus priest conducts the wedding, the couple are truly married, for the law holds such a marriage to be valid but irregular. Their intention to marry is what counts. The discovery that the service was irregular would be upsetting but not disqualifying.

Similarly, when bread and wine are placed on the altar, priest and congregation intend that the bread and wine shall be to them the body and blood of Christ, received by faith. Any bread and wine elsewhere, say on a side table, are not so perceived. Indeed, it may so happen that this 'spare' bread and wine are also on the altar, on one side of it, because in a small mud-brick church in Africa, with a dung floor and a tin or thatched roof, with crowds of children in every available space, there is no other place for it to be put. The doctrine of Intention focuses on that which is intended and leaves the rest. Its purpose is that inward sustaining of the individual and of the Christian community, whether it be in the smallest mud-brick church or the greatest cathedral of the land. By the doctrine of Extension we are to focus in a similar way on a 'setting forth', so that it is not a meandering but a focused event.

I have been helped to see more clearly how this happens by sharing in African worship in recent years. Forty years ago, during the Apartheid period in South Africa, there was considerable reluctance among most congregations to move away from the very traditional Anglican forms of worship. This was especially true of African congregations; they needed to hold onto all things Anglican including *Hymns Ancient and Modern* and Anglican chant. The Anglican Church in South Africa was the leading church in opposing Apartheid in its early years: African music is what sects and independent churches did. All this has changed. Anglican worship in South Africa is much more varied: Kudu horns are blown to welcome a new Bishop, drums and marumbas—wooded xylophones—are used on a regular basis. African composers write for an African church and this combines happily with well-known and well-loved hymns. And you do not go to church for an hour! Services of two of three hours are common, my own record being six hours, but it was *Easter Day!* Music and dance combine with an intense devotion that is very powerful.

The *intention* to worship fully is then lived out by a 'setting forth' or 'extension' that is quite different from the old anti-Apartheid struggle. From the exuberant worship, men and women go out to face all the pain and loss involved in the HIV/AIDS crisis. Homes are visited, the sick and dying cared for, respite schemes are set up, food shared. And in a great many parishes, orphans are fed and their education ensured by the provision of a school uniform. There are millions of sub-Saharan African families that are headed by a grandparent or by a teenager caring for younger siblings, and I have been into enough of their huts or tin shacks to know something of the struggle and the hopes of these young people. It is in this caring, this 'setting forth unto their whole extent' that some of the saints of our age are found.

Such 'setting forth' can be very costly; indeed sometimes 'costing not less than everything'. To pray that we may 'give and not count the cost, fight and not heed the wounds' is not a recipe for safe or easy living!

By a strange coincidence, both my parents visited Germany in the early 1930s, prior to their engagement. My father had walking holidays in the Black Forest, whilst my mother went with friends for the tercentenary production of the Oberammergau Passion Play in

1934. It was usual then to stay in the homes of the people, and my mother and her friends were lodged in the home of the man playing the part of Judas. Almost all dramatic productions of the life and passion of Christ, from the Medieval Mystery plays in England to the Oberammergau Passion are very much longer than our Gospel accounts, and all the characters have speeches and conversations that are not in Scripture, but simply based on the events. In the Oberammergau play, Judas has a large part, including one long soliloquy where he argues with himself as to what he should do. My parents returned together to Oberammergau in 1960 and called at the house where my mother had stayed. Asking after 'Judas' of 1934 they were told that playing the part had eventually turned his mind: he spent the rest of his life in a mental hospital. He had entered into the part of Judas so fully, 'setting forth himself' for a whole year, that he took on the pain and guilt of the man who handed Jesus over.

One of our Epiphany hymns has the phrase 'costly devotion'.[5] Where do we find that in the church today? Without doubt it is there in some family situations: some of the stories of the way young people, barely into their teens, spend a huge part of their young lives caring for a sick or disabled parent, are a great inspiration. Is it too much to hope that cutbacks in benefits will never affect these young carers?

I have never forgotten the impact of the 'costly devotion' of others on my own grudging acceptance of duty. I had driven the 150 miles of dirt road from the cathedral where I was based to the Mission Hospital that our church ran. I was tired and I looked forward to a bit of a lie-in the next morning, but the African priest had arranged for me to celebrate the 6.00 a.m. Communion service. I turned out pretty unwillingly, wondering who would else be there. As the half-light of dawn began to fill the chapel, I could make out some eighteen or twenty people, quietly and devoutly joining in, and in my language, for as yet I knew nothing of theirs.

It is that sort of half-hearted unwillingness to grasp the opportunities of God when he gives them, that I have always felt to be summed up in some lines of Dante. At the beginning of the first part of *The Divine Comedy (Inferno),* Virgil promises to show Dante the varying levels of hell, but Dante hangs back. Dante writes:

> As one who wills and then unwills what's willed,
> whose many thoughts can make his purpose quail
> and what's begun is quit before fulfilled:
>
> So, hesitant I stood in that dark dale:
> my thinking overshadowed my intent,
> my first, quick urge to act had no avail.[6]

By such hesitating do we ourselves miss the opportunities God gives us? For some the opportunity can be little more than a courageous demonstration of disapproval. I think of the women of the Black Sash Movement, who, for the decades of the Apartheid policy of the Nationalists, stood outside Parliament in Cape Town once a week. A similar group of Israeli women demonstrates every week in Jerusalem, against the anti-Palestinian policies of the government there. Indeed, young Israeli activists have turned to South Africa's past for the words they need to find: Apartheid, Bantustan. The silent protests, and others less silent, can be powerful examples of an interpretation of Hamlet's 'take up arms against a sea of troubles'.

There is, however, a danger we must be careful to avoid. In seeking to 'set forth ourselves unto our whole extent', in working out what a doctrine of Extension might mean for each of us individually, or what it might mean for a congregation, we could be led down the road of a desperate activism that is quite uncertain whether it is going backwards or forwards: as long as it is moving it seems that it must be all right! We all know this is not so. Both parish life and the life of each person in it can indeed reflect the eagles of the prophet Isaiah. Even a church council can rise up with wings like the eagles, as the group responds joyfully to some renewed vision, and then goes off to implement it. But more often, a church council will have a more plodding sort of glory, a 'walk and not faint' sort of style; often it will feel a bit dull—usually, though not always necessarily. Individuals are the same but we must be wary of rushing to judgement on appearances.

Once, when taking a graveside service for a man who had taken his own life, and a large urban parish had too many suicides, I knew he had faced some demons of his own, so I told the story of Sister Clotilde in A.J. Cronin's novel *The Keys of the Kingdom*. It is about a young priest in China at the time of the 1900 Boxer Rebellion. The priest and a small group of sisters are coping with an outbreak of cholera. Sister Clotilde has not been an easy person to live and work with, but she contracts the cholera. As she lies dying, the priest beside her reflects that too often we judge others by their visible defeats: God alone knows their invisible victories. The Passion of Jesus Christ is about defeat *and* victory, or it is about nothing.

3

'And all the glory of his Passion prize'

I have staked out some of the areas of indifference which we may actively or complicitly be involved with, although I should perhaps put 'inactively', as indifference is most always negative and inactive. I have tried to show how an antidote to the indifference of the world or the church might be found in a new 'setting forth' of ourselves and of the church we belong to, and that this may be as much found in the faithfulness and duty of one person or a small group than in some life-changing movement challenging the powers that be.

I am fascinated by Traherne's use of the word 'prize'. For a start, it is a verb, which is not common these days. I suppose we might say we 'prize our countryside highly', but still, as an active verb, it is fairly rare. He uses it twice in the verse before the one we are considering from the poem 'Another':

> He prizes our love with infinite Esteem.
> And seeks it so that it doth almost seem
> Even all his blessedness. His Love doth prize
> It as the only sacrifice.[7]

It occurs again in the next verse, when Traherne bids us to 'prize' God's goodness. Traherne is a poet of affirmative love and for him all creation shows it. In his poem *Thoughts* IV, he reflects:

> Could we but justly, wisely, truly prize
> These blessings, we should be above the skies.

In his *First Century*, paragraphs 46 and 47 are all about prizing:

> To have blessings and to prize them is to be in Heaven; to have them and not to prize them, is to be in Hell, I would say upon Earth … To prize blessings while we have them is to enjoy them.[8]

How much commoner in our own time is the word 'prize' as a noun, as something to win. A dozen television shows and a hundred magazines offer prizes. Traherne's offer is very different, and in a juxtaposition of words that mark him as a true poet, we are asked to prize the glory of Christ' Passion. Those well versed in St John's Gospel will find less to surprise them here, for John constantly refers to Jesus' death on the cross as his moment of glory: 'The hour has come for the Son of Man to be glorified' (John 12:23, cf. 7:39; 12:16).

In the earliest Christian centuries, there was little attempt to paint or portray Jesus on the cross, but gradually artists and sculptors, carvers of wood or ivory, embroiderers and enamellers, stained glass makers and experts in illuminated manuscripts, all made an attempt. The earliest portrayals show Jesus robed and crowned upon the cross—Christus Victor—Christ in glory, reigning from the tree. Celtic Christians in Cornwall and Wales, Brittany, Scotland and Ireland, cut their rough granite crosses with crucifixion scenes that can still be seen today, some with the robed Christ.

To mark the Millennium, The National Gallery put on the most extensive exhibition of Christian art ever seen in this country. Called *Seeing Salvation* it attracted record crowds, and the book that went with the exhibition is a constant reminder of what a thought-provoking and inspiring event this was. My own visit was marked in two ways. A mother and two children were working their way around just ahead of me and the boy of 10 or 11 was asking the most pertinent and difficult questions at almost every item, whilst his mother made a gallant attempt to combine religious knowledge and art criticism in her replies. 'Prizing the Passion' can have another meaning. We prize a fossil from a rock, a jewel from its setting; this meaning has the sense of digging away until the truth is found, is prized out, and this is what the boy was doing. Perhaps Traherne is really asking us to do the same, to really struggle with the seeming contradiction of 'all the glory of his Passion prize'.

The second incident was almost more telling. In a small room at the entrance and exit, close to .where Holman Hunt's *Light of the World.* and Salvadore Dali's *St John of the Cross* were hung, a short DVD played continuously, to tell us how the exhibition was put together and the main themes we should look out for. Standing at the back were seven or eight of the Sisters who belong to Mother Theresa's Order, founded in Calcutta but now spread around the world. They were of different races and colour, but were all in their distinctive and simple blue-bordered white saris. It came to me that for every Christian, *Seeing Salvation* could never be just something to look at; it had to be something lived, and these Sisters lived salvation, their whole way of life given to saving others, and they find the glory of the passion of Christ in the faces of the poor and the dying in Calcutta and in many other cities around the world.

Not everyone wants to recognize Christ in this way. When Peter says, on being questioned on his relationship with Jesus as he stands in the courtyard of the High Priest, 'I do not know the man', in one sense he speaks truly, for the captive figure before him is not the man of Galilee and Capernaum, of transfiguration on Mount Tabor, or of a memorable sermon on the Mount of Beatitudes. Recognizing Christ in the face of others is no easier for us, and upon recognizing pain and suffering, it is no easier to act upon it. True Christian art challenges us, as do those Sisters.

When the Bosnian War was at its worst, and when Sarajevo, a city where Muslim and Christian had lived and worked in harmony for years, was being destroyed in the bombing and fighting, I went to a Derbyshire village for their well-dressing. These decorations of the well are often, by tradition, biblical scenes; the wet clay is pricked out by the designer and teams of skilled people create the intricate designs using flower petals, bark seeds or cones. Outside the church was a representation in flowers of all the pain of Sarajevo. Children, Christian and Muslim, were kneeling with their backs to the viewer, and they, with us, looked onto the charred ruins of their city and their lives. Churches, mosques and houses were burning and collapsing. And around the border white flowers were flecked with blood-red spots, and a dove carried an olive leaf in its beak. As a work of art, it was remarkable, a statement of the pain and passion of the world, heart-breaking and prayer-inspiring. Prizing the glory of Christ's Passion, lived out in our own times, leads us to fall on our knees in both confession and adoration and then rise up with new-found strength to live the Passion in our own lives.

One of the items that did not make the National Gallery in 2000 is the *Isenheim Altarpiece,* in Colmar. In his book *Credo* the theologian Hans Küng describes the figure of Christ as portrayed there by Matthias Grünewald (1470–1528):

> his fingers are stretched out and bent, almost the most painful thing about this man of grief, and his feet are pierced by an over-large nail. His whole distorted body, covered in wounds, hangs down heavily. His head, additionally tortured by a crown of jagged thorns, has sunk on his breast. Here is unprecedented passion preaching for educated and illiterate alike.[9]

Küng goes on to write that visitors to the Museum Unterlinden in Colman may turn away, unable to face such an extreme picture of suffering. But the altarpiece is not in its proper place, although it is in a church. In the monastery chapel at Isenheim it was prayed before daily by the clergy and ordinary people, but, separated from them for safety, the poorest of the poor: lepers. Their deformities of face and finger, skin and joints would seem to be the suffering of Christ before them. But when the doors of the altarpiece were open for festivals, there the lepers would see the risen Christ, rising up, surrounded by light and colour, and still with the white grave cloth upon him and the wounds clearly seen.

Few diseases in history have quite the history of leprosy, but perhaps in our own time HIV and AIDS have taken its place, and in parts of the world, most notably in Southern Africa, these have decimated the populations of the countries there, leaving many villages and towns the preserve of bereaved grandparents and orphaned children.

My own 'work experience' took me to Southern Africa, but in my childhood it was India that dominated my young life, not by going there, but by my father spending much of the war there. Postcards came regularly and sometimes huge tins of sweets, or shirts and shorts run up by Indian tailors. Out of the first eight years of married life for my parents, six were spent at war and for four of these, my father was in India. When a sabbatical became a possibility for me (not after seven years but twenty-seven!) I felt drawn to the country of the postcards and sweets. An amazing six-week journey took me from the street children in Mumbai (Bombay) to evangelism in rural Andra Pradesh; from Madras—now Chennai—to Tamil Nadu and Madurai, 'Ooty' in the Nilgiri Hills, Cochin, Kerala and a Christian ashram. It was while staying at the Tamil Nadu Theological Seminary in Madurai that my own encounter with lepers took place.

I had been out all day, and returned to find two church wardens waiting for me. I had forgotten that they had arranged to take me to a leper colony outside the city, one which their church visited regularly and supported in various ways. We arrived as dusk was falling; I had had no time to wash; my hands were dirty; my feet dusty and worst of all I was still in my shorts, not a traditional dress for parish visiting.

The scene can only be called Dickensian: small pools of light glowed in doorways or from the tiny windows of the small houses where the lepers lived. Around fires, families cooked supper, and smoke drifted across the compound. A delegation gathered to greet and welcome me, an honoured if badly-dressed visitor. I placed my hands together in the traditional Indian greeting. One of the women placed a garland of flowers around my neck, but she had no fingers, just the stumps the leprosy had left her, and many of the other adults were the same. The glory of the flowers—had someone with no fingers made this garland of transitory beauty?—and the passion, the suffering of the people who lived in this strangely beautiful place has haunted me ever since, and it reminds us powerfully of how we prize the glory of Christ's Passion. These were the heirs of the men and women who had gazed at the suffering and deformed figure on the Isenheim Altarpiece. In England their companions in suffering would look through the leper squint that can still be seen in many of our Medieval churches. Could they glimpse any glory through that hole in stone? Or can the lepers of India today? To receive a gift of flowers from a group of lepers seems to me to be an act of glory, a moment of love that transcends all suffering.

We are so used to thinking that we, who feel that we are at least reasonably 'whole', are to give to those who suffer; when it is all reversed, we are close to 'prizing out' some of the glory of the Passion of Christ. I like to think that Traherne had this use of 'prize' also in his mind. Like a geologist on the Jurassic Coast of Dorset, or a theological equivalent of the young David Attenborough, we are to 'prize out' the truths of our faith and the glories of Christ's Passion, as others prize out a fossil from a rock. Now once we see the word 'prize' in this light, it becomes an intensely powerful concept. The glory of the Passion will not be revealed in dull preaching or facile hymns. There is work to be done, truths to be grasped and wrestled with, until, like Jacob, we too are exhausted at the break of day.

The church in England seems less sure than it was in the past about either 'grasping' or 'wrestling'. We need more of both. The most memorable prayer in our Church of England *Common Worship*, one that many of us know by heart because it is good in many ways, is the post-Communion prayer: 'Father of all, we give you thanks and praise … Keep us firm in the hope you have set before us, so we and all your children, shall be free ...'. Written originally, I believe, by Professor David Frost of an English Department in an Australian University, the prayer as it appeared in 'Series 3', precursor of the *Alternative Service Book* of 1980, read *'keep us in the hope that we have grasped'*. That is a strong image, a poetic image, a 'we have an anchor that keeps the soul' sort of image. We who set out to 'grasp', are grasped ourselves by the loving hand of God. How much weaker then is some misguided Liturgical Committee of General Synod that changed this strong image for 'keep us in the hope you have set before us'. Around the world Christians face tough challenges, persecution, loss of church property, even loss of life. They are not going to be sustained by a hope merely 'set before them'. They need a hope to grasp that enables them to prize the glory of Christ's Passion. The Church in Australia and New Zealand has wisely retained the original wording.

In the Prayer Book the 'Prayer for the Church' was—and still is—prefaced by the words 'Let us pray for the whole state of Christ's Church militant here on earth'. Most of us don't do 'militant' very well these days! However, I would have thought there were enough causes around—the hungry, the homeless, the closing of libraries, increasing food banks, dictators who slaughter their own people—for most of us to find something to be militant about, angry enough or sad enough to make either a protest or a donation towards change.

Living with apartheid in South Africa meant that very small acts that would be entirely normal elsewhere in the world, became symbols of protest—allowing an African visitor through the front door rather than sending him round to wait at the back, and allowing an African to drink from a cup that was washed and re-used rather than broken. Writing of these things so many years later they seem unreal, even surreal, so when shafts of light broke through the darkness, we could rejoice. The regular congregation I served was white and coloured: the African congregation met in the location or township, always a little way — sometimes quite a long way — from the town. The confirmation group was mixed, and as we drew near to the date when the Bishop was to come, two white parents came to see me. 'Did I know', they asked, 'that by tradition the white children were confirmed first and then the coloured'? I explained that diocesan policy was for children to be in alphabetical order, irrespective of race.

They were not entirely happy and appealed to the archdeacon who agreed with what I had said. They were regular and faithful worshippers and continued to be so, and the confirmation went well. When so many other churches were segregated, being a white Anglican in South Africa was not easy. About a year later we had a diocesan mission and our two missioners were a white priest and a black Mother Superior. As part of our week, we held a service of healing where Black and White worshipped together, shared in the laying on of hands or received it kneeling next to a Christian of a different race. When it came to a sharing of the peace, the woman who had questioned the confirmation policy, deliberately crossed the aisle—not so common then as now—to greet the Mother Superior. If I had grasped a moment of truth when it came, it was she who grasped the hope of a new South Africa. It was another twenty years in coming.

It is sometimes said that every person stands at the foot of the cross and is judged by God on their response to the one who is nailed there. But we are also judged with those who did not quite make it to the cross, but whose actions, or failure to act, ensured the death of Jesus. Pilate from the wall of his fortress represents me when I fail to have the courage of my convictions or disclaim responsibility for my actions or my indifference. Caiaphas from the window of his palace represents me when I take a worldly church too seriously and a religious system too dogmatically, when I place the church over the Kingdom of God. Judas, from under the branch of his tree, reproves me when I do not take issues of guilt, treachery, or simply failing someone seriously enough, or when I allow despair to overcome hope. These men are negative figures, but they enable us to prize more fully the glory of Christ's Passion.

4

'Who for thee lives, who for thee dies'

When a poet uses words in a particular order, we cannot always discern the reason, but we can guess that there is one and try to tease it out. Traherne might just as well have found another way of rhyming 'prize', for example:

> And all the glory of his passion prize
> Who for thee died, who for thee did rise.

Indeed, we normally speak and write of the 'death and resurrection of Jesus': we do not normally say 'the resurrection and death of Jesus'. So I suppose we have in Traherne's phrase 'who for thee lives' words that apply to the birth, life and ministry of our Lord, a life and ministry that leads to his death on the cross.

I have always believed that a parish church that kept Holy Week fully would never need a 'parish mission'—that is one of the now rather old-fashioned sort when a missioner and a team, perhaps of ordinands, 'invaded' a parish for a week. I am moving back to thinking that such a week might have a place again, especially for the good of the ordinands. But Holy Week gives us a mission opportunity every year, and how it is observed and celebrated can say a great deal about the spiritual life of the Christian community: it can indicate to a wider community whether or not we take the death and resurrection of Jesus as seriously and as joyously as we should. And it can combine an intense prayerfulness *from* the committed—sharing the Daily Offices on Monday–Wednesday, and being at the Watch late on the Thursday night. These are times when the church witnesses to itself—with extraordinary opportunities for helping people outside the life of the Church to catch a glimpse of what it all means to us.

On Palm Sunday as I knew it in a village, the donkey would start at the chapel for the Palm Sunday readings and hymns, and then lead a procession to the parish church for the Passion Gospel and Communion. In a town parish we started at the Co-op! Here I found that over the years we would have almost as many at the Palm Sunday service as on Easter Day. In town and village alike, Good Friday is increasingly marked by ecumenical processions of witness, clergy and people behind a cross, perhaps stopping at intervals for 'stations', and ending in a church or chapel or in the middle of the shops. And it is often a day for a dramatic presentation of the last hours of Jesus' life, leading up to the crucifixion, and as it is a working day for many, if such a drama is portrayed between 12.00 p.m. and 3.00 p.m., it can be experienced by many. In recent years there has been a growth in town-centre passion plays, including Trafalgar Square. Perhaps when we read the Passion Gospel, we could add a couple of words, saying 'Simon from Cyrene *in Libya*' to remind ourselves and Libyans that their country was a great centre of Christian life and witness for several hundred years, along with most of North Africa; Egypt, Syria, Turkey, Iraq. And perhaps we need to remember that well established churches can almost completely vanish, as happened in much of North Africa after the spread of Islam.

The phrase 'Who for thee lives, who for thee dies' helps us to hold onto the fact that we celebrate Good Friday in the knowledge of Easter to come, and that we celebrate Easter with the cross in pride of place in our churches. It was John Donne, in the same century as Traheme, who said in a sermon: 'His Christmas and his Good Friday are but morning and evening of the same day'. Traherne's line, 'Who for thee lives, who for thee dies', has the same sense of wholeness, reflecting perhaps the great cry from the cross in St John, 'It is finished', meaning of course, the work is accomplished. God's glory is achieved in this suffering love, and down the Christian centuries, acts of suffering love have re-affirmed what God was doing in Christ, reconciling the world.

Amongst the many tensions, discussions, arguments and disagreements of the past hundred years and more, has been the whole area of 'crime and punishment': our laws, our police, our judicial system, our treatment of prisoners and our care of their victims. For three years I served as a prison chaplain in an establishment for women prisoners and as a girls' borstal. The regime was reasonably 'light touch'; girls could, and did, abscond, for doors were usually unlocked, and the whole emphasis was on education and rehabilitation, which could be other words for reconciliation. Some of the women, who came from Holloway, had been convicted of the murder or manslaughter of one of their children, but most for less heinous crimes. The girls were 16–18, and almost all came from the toughest areas of our inner cities: London, Cardiff, Glasgow, Liverpool. Many of those areas have been transformed, but we have more people than ever in our prisons. Some of the girls would usually be in the church choir, and some asked to be confirmed. The Borstal was a splendid old house so we met in a room with a blazing log fire. No doubt some of the girls had helped to cut the logs as they spent time on the estate or in the gardens; at least one champion pig-breeder was an inmate here! I had prepared my discussion and teaching for the small group of girls, and we began with us all reading St Luke's *Parable of the Prodigal Son.* Whatever it was that I had planned to talk to them about had to be left to another time. The idea that God could be like a loving father, waiting, looking expectantly for the errant young man, came as a belief they struggled with. Too many of them came from families where they were not going to be welcomed back; too many of them had abusive fathers to make the idea of God as a 'loving father' difficult to grasp.

In those days we were able to exercise a 'variable sentence'; each month we would sit round a table, discuss the progress of each girl. The statutory sentence was normally seven months, but we had the power to extend this by another two or three months. This was always done for the girls we felt could really be helped by being with us a bit longer, who were making progress and who, we felt, would be less likely to re-offend if we had them for a bit longer, or if we needed more assurance from the Probation Service that their care on their return could be better done a month or two later. I have watched girls in tears embracing their warders as they leave, knowing that some aspects of life at home were going to be far worse than life had been here. How many of the girls who were confirmed or in the choir followed up their church membership on their return home I shall never know. What I do know is that how a society deals with its offenders is of paramount importance, and that the church has a ministry for those whom the state sends to prison, and to the staff, who have the very demanding job of caring for them. The church should also play a very supportive role for those who are the victims of crime.

Because most of us live into old age, and old age is older than is used to be, many people die in hospital or in some form of care home. Much as we may hope to die peacefully in our own bed, in extreme old age we may need more care—and bluntly—more practical equipment than the average home or average family member can supply, and if both of a couple are in their later 80s, caring is not easy, probably not feasible. We may want, deeply desire, that we can translate 'who for thee lives, who for thee dies' into living together and, if not dying together, at least one of a married couple dying with the other present. The same can be said for an adult child who is probably also a pensioner, facing the death of a parent. Nevertheless, fewer deaths occur within the family or even with a family member present. It is no use berating or blaming ourselves for this: it is simply the cost we pay for living much longer, which most of us will hopefully do and with some degree of joy. In these circumstances, the living and dying of Jesus Christ can still transform the event.

When a child or young adult dies, it is all very different and friends and family will struggle even more to make sense of what has happened, and to see how the living and dying of Jesus Christ can help in the context of this pain. As a priest it is one thing to be at the bedside of an elderly person who is dying; quite another when it is say, a teenager. It requires special qualities which, I fear, few of us have. Yet, our faith is in the life, death and resurrection of a young man of 33, so we have the history and resources for dealing with the dying of the young.

It is a tragic truth that the twentieth century saw the dying of more young people, in their teens and twenties, than many a previous century. Just as we began to see fewer children dying—in all my past parishes the burial registers averaged a child a page until well into the twentieth century—now there have been two World Wars and a great number of lesser wars, and the involvement of our own country is indicated by the fact that there is only one year in the twentieth century when a British service-person did not die in action. Perhaps a lesser known fact is that by ratio to population, Australia had the highest death toll of any of the Allies in the two World Wars.

A remarkable picture by Stanley Spencer covers the east wall of Sandham Memorial Chapel, near Burghclere in Hampshire. Spencer had spent the whole of the 1914–18 War as a medical orderly, and almost all the chapel walls are covered in paintings—oil on canvas—of scenes from medical and military life. He had already painted his 'Resurrection, Cookham' by the time he started work on the chapel, but it does little to prepare us for the impact of the Sandham Chapel east wall. Everywhere soldiers are arising from their graves, carrying or framed by their simple white cross, the sort of cross probably put up at the time of death in the trenches, rather than the later headstones we know in War Cemeteries today. The mules of an ammunition limber arise too, with their driver. And in the far distance, a soldier is handing his cross to the seated figure of Christ. On the left the rising comrades greet each other. What could it be like to celebrate at this altar, facing this wall?

One of the strongest themes of Easter for me has always been that the risen Christ is still the wounded Jesus: he says, 'Behold my hands and my side'. He says this too of our living and dying and the living and dying of a broken, wounded humanity. No wounds, no resurrection. In a world such as ours, in a past hundred years such as ours, only a wounded figure of Christ can begin to answer, and to challenge, our questing and our doubting.

Many years ago I had three parishes in Kent: the churches and villages had the North Downs and the County Town to their rear, while they faced out onto the Weald, and towards the distant English Channel. Down in the Weald lived Mr and Mrs W, and every month I took them their Holy Communion. They had been married 64 years. In 1918 Mrs W was summoned by the military authorities and was given permission to go to France, where her husband was seriously ill. On the boat she fell in with an older woman who was going to see her son, aged 18, who had been badly injured when flying a plane. It turned out that the two men were in adjacent beds. The next day the boy died and Mrs W decided to go to the funeral. Beforehand she went into the nearby woods to gather some twigs, moss, leaves and wild flowers, and made them into a crude form of a wreath. On turning up at the vast graveyard, she found two coffins. She placed the wreath on the boy's coffin and went to stand with the mother, there being no mourners for the other dead man. Then the mother stepped forward, took the wreath and broke it in two, placing half on each coffin. Amidst war and all the pity of war, this broken wreath has always seemed to me to be a symbol of love in all our human brokenness, a moment of hope in so much of our human pain. Half a wreath says more than a whole one ever can. If a whole wreath is a symbol of God's eternal love, half a wreath is a reminder that his eternal love comes only through the cross and the wounds of Christ.

When a teacher took a class of children round my parish church, one little girl stood looking intently at the figure of Jesus on the rood screen cross. Then turning to the teacher she said 'They say he escaped later'. She may have grown up to find that she was announcing a very early Christian heresy, but most of us have to grow up to know that escape from our human condition, from all the worldly pain and cruelty, can only be achieved by the one who did not escape himself, who went through the Valley of Death, and who does so with each of us.

Few of us are called to the heights of great sacrifice or nobility of life. Most of us who acknowledge the title 'Christian' lead lives of comparative ordinariness. Any 'passion prizing' we may do will have to be within the 'daily round, the common task', but as the poet says, that itself

> Would furnish all we ought to ask;
> Room to deny ourselves, a road
> To bring us daily nearer God.[10]

I have always found this understanding of 'being where we are' and God using that circumstance, that situation, most beautifully expressed in a poem by Charles Williams. He is often called the 'third Inkling', a member of the group that met weekly in Oxford to read each other the latest chapter of the book they were writing, before, during and after the Second World War. C. S. Lewis and J.

R. R. Tolkien remain well known and well read—even now, well filmed—but Charles Williams less so. He wrote seven remarkable novels, several fine theological works including one on 'the history of the Holy Spirit' in the Church, at least six books of poetry, and some verse plays. His play 'Thomas Cranmer' was written for the Friends of Canterbury Cathedral, for whom T. S. Eliot and Dorothy Sayers also wrote. A lesser known work by Williams is called *The Rite of the Passion* and it contains this poem which I have known for almost as long as my four lines from Thomas Traherne:

Who will be gentle, blithe, and debonair
  even when the miracle is wholly ceased?
who will make courtesy his daily care,
  whether he serve the greatest or the least?
who will attend his cousins with goodwill,
  even though his own heart faint for need thereof?
though duteous kindness be his only skill
  who late was vassal and blood-brother to Love?
Watch for Love's coming—but in others' need,
  ravage not the wild wilderness for a sign,
but in your nearest neighbourhood give heed
  to what least light may on those neighbours shine.
All else is Love's—this only must be given—
  A gate, a place, an opening meet for heaven.[11]

Selected Poems

Jan van Eyck, The Arnolfini Portrait (1434), National Gallery, London. Public domain, image reproduced from Wikimedia Commons.

Mrs Arnolfini Replies to her Husband. Van Eyck 1434

This is serious moment in their lives
so grave looks are in order for Van Eyck,
and both Arnolfinis have to strive
to hold a hand, resist a smile
or ask, "Why did you leave that apple
on the sill, my dear?" "Ah sir,
perfection is a doubtful game in love;
your sombre gown fur trimmed
and that enormous hat I told you not to wear.
My sumptuous bed and crimson hangings,
my best green dress with my expectant child
all speak of our prosperity in life. But love
is not so tidy everywhere; it scatters round the rooms
of all our lives the unexpected and the trite,
enough to say, wealth and perfection may not last
and some untidiness recalls, even for us,
in this grand room, that love has normal moments;
two pairs of shoes left lying, as to say,
This is a home, things happen, get left out,
and you who love order and control
have lost it here". In the small mirror
between them both, the artist is witness
to a less tidy love that is complete,
their seriousness made just more human
by the small dog at their feet.

On a French Church Clock Being Electrified for The Hours and The Angelus

This bell is a remembrance of times
when people knew and had in mind
some purpose of its sound, its chimes.
Now there's forgetfulness. We wind

our church towers' clocks, or set each
automatically so no complaint
can give an opportunity to teach
some reason for the sound. Quaint

custom carries on where we let be
real observation of this building's cause;
an entry into time and space of he
who sourced its function and our laws.

Houses

Sometimes there are towns, houses together
that seem to be in the wrong place,
set down to inconvenience fields or weather,
or interrupting the trees they have to face.

Some houses grow from the landscape
like their surrounding hedge or wall,
but others impose their presence, as a rape
causes permanent damage to us all.

Studland

Only where the cranesbill clinging near the pathway
and isolated clumps of cowslip manage to subsist,
dandelion and buttercup relieve the green green grass swathe,
sea-birds quietly call from an early summer mist.

Perpetuating myths, small boats ply the sea lanes
with their coal and their peacocks and their cheap tin trays,
while the well-to-do are sailing and the less-to-do are walking
and lovers are lingering above the white cliffed bays.

Cromford Mill

Child labour was a norm. Twelve hours a day,
parents and children created thread to loom.
Warp and weave of their existence. Life
is too big a word for how they lived.

Child labour has gone. Twelve hours a day
no union man would stand. We use a broom,
such chimneys there are. Our little coal
comes from few men and their machines,

and then from imports every day. Columbian minors
underground; while the loom uses
small fingers in the East for cloth
and carpets, and our conscience ease.

Jacobs Well – Jesus Well – "And did those feet"?

Wells do not move. Stone walls
may be rebuilt – a house, a church,
a palace. Wells remain. Research
enables us to sit where water falls,
from jars and buckets raised again
as once they quenched one Man's thirsty pain.

Builders needed tin and Joseph came
following Phoenician traders' roads
in the sea, whose ship-filled loads
gave Cornwall's miners world-wide fame.
Maybe the boy and he sat on this hill
And drank the water we drink still.

Note: Jesus Well is on a golf course in North Cornwall.

A Church Times Advert: "St Mary Redcliffe, Bristol will be Floodlit this Christmas"

Ah! St Mary Redcliffe saved
from dark oblivion night after night.
"Now permanently floodlit" raved
the advert for your Christmas Services.

Maybe some shepherd on the Mendip Hills
will see refracted glory in the sky.
Wise men will ponder on "Who pays the bills"?
and purchase shares in Electricity.

Mount Grace Priory

Walking through your domesticated ruins
I feel at home. Rather than poverty
simple simplicity is marked, but not uncomfortable,
that is, until the riders came.

All of us need to be disturbed, but not as much as these;
disturbed, not destroyed.
We owe you scholarship, books and memory – important for a faith.
A skill in gardening, medicine and herbs.
Perhaps town planning owes you thanks,
Houses around a gracious square.
Moorland farming and some breeds of sheep.
Commercial agricultural debts the king forgot to pay.

We sweep away what we have deemed corrupt –
monastic orders, despots' power,
Governments in hock to left or right,
But what was good takes longer to re-build.
Some, like this, still lie in silent ruins to rebuff
some zealots quest for power or purity or cash.

Perhaps it's only ruins that remind us
of all that we have lost and lose.

Here you showed the world its need
to keep a private space – a lawn, a fire,
some flowers, some decent plumbing too:

but also how to care, for land, for learning
and for the infirm,
and how to pray, the quest too many have
not set upon, which these warm stones recall us to.

Stranger

Into the empty café comes
a stranger, as if his home
were here. And I resent
the casual air, the coarse
and foreign tone, the hum
as if he owned or had a share
and claimed his interest here.

Is it perhaps that his home
is here, all others having resented
his presence in their town?
The callous air, the clipped
and county tone, the spare
glance that exhausts our interest.
When no-one talks, you hum.

From Westminster Bridge: the New Foundations of St Thomas' Hospital

Was the creation of the world like this?
No bliss, but the noise of God's finger-nail drills
carving out hollows in the land,
his hand to grab the mud
of which he made mountains of men
to move when faiths new fingers drilled again?
His craned arm pulled a river's bed
and spat the water's ebb with "Be thou made."
So, holding high foundations in his hand
He shared his subsequent creating work with Man.

In the Church: Mareham-on-the-Hill

Here where restorers' zeal has left untouched
the painted box-pews where our fathers' faith
bid them pray face to face, each door being latched,
adding their hid "Amen" to all the vicar saith.

The flickering oil-lamps gut and flame again,
The hoarse-voiced verger stirs with verbal prod,
hoping each child, each farmer's wife to train
back to the altar, travelling home to God.

A Norwich Church with Alternative Use

Here where the Word of God was read aloud
whether inspiring or uninspiring tone,
paperbacks and books are all allowed –
words can be bought for pence and carried home,
whereas before, relying on what we heard,
we carried in our hearts and minds the Word.

And where an altar silently proclaimed
by size and prominence that it was here
something significant took place that framed
our lives, where cup and bread were dear;
now inconspicuous tables fill the void
and coffee cups and saucers are employed.

And where a certain silence could be found
to question all our chattering of the street
the space is filled with stalls on which are bound
the sacrifices that we call antique;
while all the faith that sacrifice fulfils
is lost amidst the clatter of the tills.

The Best Wine

"You have kept the best wine until now" he cried
and lifted the cup to his lips.
"You have wined and dined us in splendour and tried
to keep us from drinking this."
And the guests laughed as wedding guests do
when they've had a few drinks and they wished they were through.
Does the Bridegroom's father still keep
the best wine in Cana of Galilee now?

"You have kept the best wine until now" he cried
and lifted the cup to his lips.
"I have wined them and dined them in love and in haste,
and they will remember this."
And the soldiers laughed as they walked the path
and they'd had a few drinks too,
for the Bridegroom's father had kept
the best wine till Gethsemane now.

Cyprus Lemon

Take between your minaretted finger
and the tiled dome of your thumb,
this lemon in an old blue bowl.

The tasselled fez cries accusation
up to the blackening chimney pot,
"Divide the lemon with a blade."

"Carry the rifle in a prayer mat."
"Keep arms behind the icon-screen."
Crush all the lemon's yellowness.

Slaughter upon forgotten hillsides
for the revenging of the dead.
This lemon's bitter juice runs red.

Written in the winter of 1962/3. Ten years later the Turkish invasion of Cyprus took place, and the island has remained divided.

Boy's Song

In the Spring new spears gleam
shooting the earth no point
has ever pierced through stone
twig leather-jacket worm
and ungreened soil
as my small army
beauty-to-be-born
by my first hope filled
newness holding future.

Summer the sea-licked
newness of the sand
no foot no hand
touched or traversed the wrinkled skin
until I came at noon
to watch and follow the begging waves
that cleaned the beach
of packet tin and ground
the bottles into tiny jewels.

Born in cathedral candelabrum
conkers are Autumn's newness gold
heavens nuggets falling or forced
into the trampled grass and marked
by fingerprints of God
who cradled them with care
before bestowing to impatient hands
a kingdom of a little while
the glistening schoolboy sovereignty.

Winter the old white newness
of the crystalline snow
and where I go
new giant feet no foot
has ever trod
marked and imprinted
where in a past age nothing held
but cold death's preservation
and the white breath of God.

Graverse for a Churchyard Cat

Walk tall and proudly through the grass
and stalk the ghosts of the dead men past,
who lie down deep beneath long stones
that cast long shadows over bones
of vole and mouse, gold-crest and wren
you buried in long grasses when
they came within death's sharp embrace
that sprung from your tombstone look-out place.

Memorial

"There must be a shrine" she said,
"That is entirely mine.
A place where flowers grow,
Where I may go
To weep and lay my head."

"There must be a stone" she said,
"So that his name is known.
A place where children come;
perhaps where some
may weep and lay their head."

Remembrance

We are lucky to have old men.
Some have died in the cause of war.
They said the cause was peace
but of course the only victor
in the end is war,
self defeating, all devouring,
leaving those who should be old men now
in trenches and dugouts.
We are lucky to have old men.

We are lucky to have young men.
Some have died in the cause of peace.
Not here where hard-won freedom holds,
But elsewhere and in other places
where our assumptions of truth and justice
have no validity. There fortress fear,
mistrust, and unambiguous hate
run rampant through society.
We are lucky to have young men now.

Young men should guard the privilege
of becoming old.

Mary and the Shepherd Boy

We brought a lamb, homely,
After the eerie night,
Some goat's milk and a reed pipe.

We found the shed, draughty
to hold a birthday night,
so we gave a fleece, and light.

As I held up the lantern, brightly,
to see the crib-bound child,
I saw her hand drip blood.

"Blood from birth?" I cried
"– I watch lambs born at night –
I shall attend your hurt."

"Oh no!" she laughed, "Nothing -
a splinter from the crib;
it might have hurt the child."

I touched her bleeding hand.
"Who'd have believed" I said
"Such wounds could come from wood."

I held his unharmed hand, gently.
"As boy and man he'll wound -
How will you hold him then?"

"Then" she sighed, "Are birth and death
wounds to bring our healing?"
And as the baby laughed, we cried.

Aberfan

We said "Let the mountains fall on us"
    in the Gospel today,
"And let the hills cover us" we pray.

Cover us, earth in our mourning,
    our labours' symbol jest;
raise no mounds of memorial or rest.

Follow in the earth the long line downward
    under to the hill
with a fierce destructive cross to fill,

while death's cold fingers spring and touch
    one town's soul,
let the continuing world cremate their coal.

Arnhem

Tense waiting in the air
no silence, but the roar
of engines to accompany the prayer
to take them down to the unknown.

Now it is known:
Arnhem is our name.
Farmers of centuries have prepared
this long flat land for our burying.

He fell with them,
dead from all the clouds;
he and the others bringing
each his own shroud.

Loss

She laid the table, placed the cups
with care and cake beside the chair,
little remembering how she sups
in singular. Suddenly aware
that all she did is halved again,
replaces the china on the shelf
regretting it could cause such pain.

Goodbye at St Austell Station

A solemn sight this often made farewelling;
grave almost smiles that seem to see us
all away to some new destination,

concern or some regret perhaps foretelling;
parent or lover saddened or anxious,
or old and unresolved recrimination

from some long past familial indwelling.
Beyond a look, gesture or word to free us,
we slowly move beyond our resolution.

Mobile Phone

We keep in constant contact, you and I,
endless communication by mobile ear to ear,
yet never ask the question that we fear,
why we so seldom see things eye to eye.

Kosovo. Helston Flora Day 1999

(It rained throughout the Children's Dance so that the dye in the flowers in their hair ran onto their clothes. A man in the crowd said, "It looks like a battlefield").

We wore bright flowers in our hair, as ever,
to dance our greeting to the Spring and Summer:
And as rain fell we danced our way, together,
till all our red flowers bled, and drummer
with persistent martial beat persuaded
our dancing battleground. Feet dismembered
may mark memorial to the towns degraded,
and children with more real wounds remembered.

The Last Remembrance Sunday of the Twentieth Century

Boy's Voice
We are young, we are young -
We creep, we walk, we hide, we run
across the veld against the Boer,
out of the trenches to kill the Hun -
and James and Michael fall down, done!
and then jump up, for they pretend
their dying at this centuries end.

Man's Voice
We are young, but not so young -
we creep, we walk, we hide, we run
across the veld against the Boer,
out of the trenches to kill the Hun:
through jungles, over sand, under sun
in Sicily, Normandy, Burma and more:
through Atlantic seas or tracered skies,
on Belfast streets or Falkland Isles -
And James and Michael fall down, done.
They jump not up, do not pretend
their dying to this century's end.

Conceiving Words in our Womb

Conceiving word in our womb
smokily drifting across the mind's eye
a hard birth to die
to be bound for ever in a verbal tomb.

Words caught in the thin passage of time
miscarried in unconnected lines,
as exploding mines,
refusing the form of verse or rhyme.

Not to be drawn out with desire or pain
but desperately catching a line here or there,
as if all the air
were suddenly full of the silent words again.

Child and Mother – Treliske Hospital

There is a moment to walk hand in hand,
a mother and her son can stand
quite unselfconscious of the cord or strand
of love that holds them still together.

Later another will hold his hand in hers,
still both oblivious how the world observes
lovers and laughter, enfleshed hopes and fears
of love that holds them both together.

Small hands clasp fingers until size
allows them freedom to be separate and eyes
alone can hope a daughter's wise
in the exchange of hands you've made together.

A moment comes when the first hand is all
that dying memories can retrieve, recall,
and son and mother in a moment's thrall
enact the contact they once had together.

In a Seaside Café at Gorran Haven

I'm surprised how much they have to say,
husbands and wives, each in their own way,
at the seaside café table day after day.
I would have expected it to be more so at night
when lovers must confirm by hearing and by sight
that each is much more likely to be right.
After long years, you'd think they'd know by now
and in some silence reaffirm their vow.

The Mary Magdalene Frontal in the Morning Chapel, Lincoln Cathedral

Only the tumbling hair, bright jewelled
shines against the black material
of a Laudian Front. And near the floor
an equal jewelled jar to make a ferial
day festive with sacrificial love. More
is unknown, save maybe that encounter
with a gardener, straw-hatted in some art,
equally untouched by her or us.
Only the hair and the unbroken jar apart
recall us to our own unbroken heart.

Our Holiday

We really looked forward to the change.
It would be a complete break from the stress at work
and all that seemed wrong with our country.
When the children heard we were going to an island,
where they could play on the beach and learn to swim,
they were so excited! Our expectation was high.

What we did not expect was that
we would have to jump into the sea and walk to the beach,
as if we were an invading army.

Glastonbury

Leaves lie scattered on a lawn
that marks a pattern for our lives -
stark twigs and branches wind swept, shorn
beside a tree whose blossom thrives.
Perhaps this tree is but a thorn,
twice blossoming its love survives

Lindisfarne Priory

Pillars of faith support no roof of doubt.
Saints leave an open archway into God,
clear as the sky between leaves out
our loss, our lack, our endless questioning,
until the long long causeway of our lives
is flooded with the love of Christ alive.

Notes to the Four Talks

[1] Thomas Traherne, 'Another', in Traherne, *Poems, Centuries and Three Thanksgivings*, ed. Anne Ridler (London: Oxford University Press, 1966), 59, spelling modernized.
[2] Graham Greene, *The Comedians* (London: Bodley Head, 1966), 283.
[3] T.S. Eliot, *Murder in the Cathedral*, in *The Complete Poems and Plays of T.S. Eliot* (London: Faber, 1969), 251.
[4] John Clare, *The Later Poems of John Clare 1837–64*, ed. Eric Robinson and David Powell (Oxford: Oxford University Press, 1984), 396–7.
[5] Hymn, 'Brightest and best of the sons of the morning' by Reginald Heber.
[6] Dante, *The Inferno* Canto 2, ll. 37–42. Translated by Paul S. Fiddes.
[7] Traherne, 'Another', 59, spelling modernized.
[8] Traherne, *The First Century*, 46–7, in Traherne, *Poems*, 185, spelling modernized.
[9] Hans Küng, *Credo* (London: SCM Press, 1993), 66.
[10] Hymn, 'New every morning is the love', by John Keble.
[11] Charles Williams, 'The Rite of the Passion', in Charles Williams, *Three Plays* (London: Oxford University Press, 1931), 167–8.

Printed in Great Britain
by Amazon

46577977R00050